QUESTIONS

A Journal for the Exploration of Oneness

QUESTIONS

A Journal for the Exploration of Oneness

by
Brian G. O'Rourke

SUNSTONE
PRESS

SANTA FE

Illustrations by William Shedd

Sunstone books may be purchased for educational, business, or sales
promotional use. For information please write: Special Markets Department, Sunstone
Press, P.O. Box 2321, Santa Fe, New Mexico 87504-2321.

FIRST EDITION

10 9 8 7 6 5 4 3 2 1

Library of Congress Cataloging-in-Publication Data:

O'Rourke, Brian G., 1952–
Questions: a journal for the exploration of oneness/by Brian G. O'Rourke.—1st ed.
    p. cm.
ISBN: 0-86534-334-9
    1. Meditations. 2. Spiritual journals—Authorship. I. Title.

BL624.2 .O65 2001
291.4'32—dc21

                                                2001042976

Published in

SUNSTONE PRESS
Post Office Box 2321
Santa Fe, NM 87504-2321 / USA
(505) 988-4418 / *orders only* (800) 243-5644
FAX (505) 988-1025
www.sunstonepress.com

This book is dedicated to the love
of my three children,
Craig, Jennifer, Ryan.

May you appreciate, challenge and
enjoy your spiritual journey to the
Oneness of God.
May you always know God's love.

In this life,
I have loved no one more than you.

QUESTIONS

Throughout my life from the youngest of age, there have been endless questions about religion, my relationship with God and my spirituality. Questions that have challenged my human logic, my spiritual awaking and my inward sense of what may actually be. Questions that have caused an uncomfortableness for teachers, religious leaders and traditional adults, while providing me with a perspective (a belief) of this human life and what may follow the human experience.

I have found the need to challenge (not to condemn) the interpretations of the beliefs of others, the fear based structure of religion, the purpose of my spirituality, the journey or journeys needed to find the path to God's love, and the importance of the love for all mankind—especially those I have known as friends and family.

I have revealed in the next few pages, the accumulation of many questions that I have experienced and struggled with— as I journey through this gift that God has given—this gift we know as life.

I do not offer any answers. The answers will come from The God you love and the willingness to listen deeply to the creation known as you. God has created "who you truly are." May you find the answers.

May you know the blessings and guidance of God.

—Brian G. O'Rourke

QUESTIONS

If you came face to face with God
and could ask God any question,
what would the question be?

Are you, would you, be prepared
to listen, accept and truly feel
God's response?

❦

Thoughts:

Are the "souls" of mankind,
the children,
the offspring,
the sons and daughters
of God?

❦

Thoughts:

Is God all knowing? All loving?

Was mankind truly created
in the image and likeness
of God?

❦

Thoughts:

If mankind truly was created in
the image and likeness of God,
why would God have created anything
that would be judged "bad or sinful"?

In religious teachings,
why is it taught we are sinners?

❦

Thoughts:

Did God give mankind
the gift of "total freedom"?

Why would God give us freedom to
make choices, that someday would be
judged by God, so that the results
of our choices may cause our soul
damnation for eternity?

🕊

Thoughts:

Is God a judgmental God?
A revengeful God?
An egotistical God?
Is God only a God of love?

❦

Thoughts:

Does God have needs?

Does God need anything from…
You?
Me?
Us?

What would God need
from all of mankind?

❦

Thoughts:

Is not the birth of a newborn child
a gift of the purity of God—the
innocence and wholesomeness of life?

Why do we as parents, as teachers, as
a society, continue to inflict such
an innocence—such a purity
with prejudice and intolerance?

Thoughts:

Did God create everything?

Did God create "demons"?
Or, could mankind have created
its own demons?

Why would either create a negative
aspect to a spiritual journey?

❦

Thoughts:

Does God truly judge us following
the death of our body?

Do we judge ourselves?

Is there ever a consequence or punishment
for our choices in life?

❦

Thoughts:

Does God forgive us for our
"wrong" choices
or do we forgive ourselves?

How many times may we be
forgiven?

❧

Thoughts:

Must we forgive others? Why?

In order to forgive others, would
we not first have to make a judgement
about another and/or their actions?

By what authority, what "right,"
do we have to judge others?

❦

Thoughts:

In this human experience
why has mankind found the "need"
or the "right" to judge others
and/or condemn others for their
individual personal beliefs or choices?

❦

Thoughts:

Does Hell exist?

If Hell exists, what truly is Hell?

If Hell exists, where is Hell?

Why would God (for any reason) damn
God's creation to Hell for eternity?

❧

Thoughts:

Who decides what is "right"
and/or
what is "wrong"?

And why?

What is "sin"?

Who decides what is sin?

🐓

Thoughts:

If there was
"unconditional acceptance"
of all that appears to be different,
unique and challenging
in the ways in which life is lived,

would "forgiveness" be necessary?

❦

Thoughts:

Is it possible for mankind to be
separate or separated from the
God of our creation?

❦

Thoughts:

Why do most religions teach that
we must fear the Wrath of God?

If God truly loves us unconditionally,
what need would exist to have fear
of our Creator?

❦

Thoughts:

God,
having created the heavens and
the earth and all life upon this
earth, did not God create all
mankind equal?

🕊

Thoughts:

On the assumption that God's love
for all mankind is equal,
then why would mankind
"in the name and love of God,"
teach prejudice, declare war, hurt in
many ways the life of others based on
the origin of a person's birth, the
color of skin, the language spoken or
the individual beliefs of one person or
nation versus another?

❦

Thoughts:

What is more significant,
the word of God, or
the experiences of God?

Mankind cannot change the
experiences of God.
However, has mankind actually depicted
the experiences of God through its
interpretation and expression of the
"word of God"?

❧

Thoughts:

Are the human experiences of
some souls challenged differently
than others?

Why are some "souls" born
into a human existence of comfort,
wealth, opportunity while others
experience poverty, hunger, illness,
war/destruction or suffering of any kind?

❦

Thoughts:

Why do some children die young?

Why?

🌱

Thoughts:

Is not
the soul of the female person
equal in the eyes and love of God,
to that of the soul of
the male person?

❦

Thoughts:

Why,
in most organized religions is the
female restricted in her ability to serve
her God and/or religion,
based on the "position or rank"
she may acquire in the organized
structure of that religion?

❦

Thoughts:

Is there "one true religion"
of the God /Creator of all mankind?

If so,
would not that religion have to be
merciful, loving, understanding
and generally kind and accepting
to all souls of mankind
whether or not that "soul" claims itself
to be a member or follower
of that religion?

❦

Thoughts:

Are we a "spiritual being" having a
human experience?

Or, a "human being" waiting for a
spiritual existence?

❦

Thoughts:

Does mankind have but one life to live?
One spiritual life or one human life?

Which life, "spiritual or human"
was created first, and why?

🏺

Thoughts:

How many "lives" are we able to
experience until we understand our ·
purpose for which God has created us?

How many "lives" are we able to
experience until we truly
experience the path to
God's love?

❦

Thoughts:

How do we truly live the journey
of our spirituality when consistently
challenged by the (negative) influences of
this human life?
Are there negative influences?
Are the influences (negative or otherwise)
just our perception of choice,
or judgmental views of life?

❦

Thoughts:

When we make a promise
"in the name and love of God,"
are there any circumstances that could
prevent us from fulfilling that promise?

Will God—does God
accept and understand our choice not to
fulfill a promise made in God' name?

❧

Thoughts:

When two or more individuals are unable
to "get along," or find the goodness in
each other, why must it be
the habit of humans (more often than not)
to exist with a dislike or hatred or revenge
or jealousy or destructiveness of each other?

If we believe
in God and in the ways of God
how would this be possible?

❦

Thoughts:

Why do we not experience love for,
and of, everyone?

Does God not love all souls?

Is our human love limited to just
the souls of a few people?

❦

Thoughts:

Will God for any reason
hold back God's love, acceptance
compassion, or forgiveness
from the creation known as mankind?

Do we ever, and if so why
would we, hold back our love, acceptance,
compassion and forgiveness from others?

🌺

Thoughts:

Much of our energy, effort, worry,
discipline and time is spent creating
a living—the means to survive
on this earth.

What does it mean to create
a life worth living?
Do we understand the difference—
the importance of a life versus a living?

❦

Thoughts:

Where does human "fear" come from?

In our "spiritual life" do we experience
spiritual fear?

❧

Thoughts:

Why is mankind taught to fear death?

Is it not only the death of the
human body that we experience?

Is there not truth in the belief that
our "soul" is the "offspring" of God
and therefore will live eternally?

❦

Thoughts:

Is it the death of the human body,
or the process of death of the body
that we fear?

Is the death of the body
just the end of human life?

Or a beginning?

Or a continuation of our
spiritual journey?

❦

Thoughts:

Must we or should we live
our human life experience based solely
on the structure and disciplines of
an organized religion?

What part does our spirituality—
the inward truth and guidance
of our soul—
play in our inevitable journey?

❦

Thoughts:

Is it not possible that God created us
so that we would create our own
human experiences?

Could the purpose of these human
experiences help us discover our truest gift?

Our purest identity?
Our divine spirituality?
Our oneness with God?

❦

Thoughts:

Have you ever experienced
a reversal of a belief or some knowledge
you held sacred?

Have you ever experienced,
what you thought or were taught was true—wasn't,
and what you thought or were taught
wasn't true—was?

❦

Thoughts:

Who or what controls our every thought?

Does God?

Do we individually?

How are our negative and/or positive
thoughts created?

How are our thoughts of love
and/or hate created?

❦

Thoughts:

Are there Prophets among us today?

Are there "true masters" of God's love
living and teaching among us today?

Are you a Prophet?

Are you a Master of God's love?

Will you ever be a Prophet/Master?

❦

Thoughts:

When we pray,
does it matter how we pray?

Does God want or require or prefer
our prayers to be structured?

In prayer, is listening not just as important
as the expression of our personal thoughts?

❦

Thoughts:

The Bible and other religious doctrine
are read by many as the basis
of God's teachings.
What other ways has God communicated
God's message to mankind?
Has God continuously communicated
to all of us throughout
the past two thousand years?

❦

Thoughts:

What is love?

In the human sense?

In the spiritual sense?

Thoughts:

Are there questions we are afraid
to ask—to explore?

Questions about God?

Questions about ourselves?

Questions about our spiritual/life's journey?

Thoughts:

Will we ever live a life upon this earth
in total commitment to the love of God,
so that we will live a life of
appreciation and love of our
neighbor—of all mankind?

How and when
will mankind best experience
and
truly know the Love of God?

❦

Thoughts:

Who amongst mankind will have
the courage, the consistency in love
and
the understanding of spirituality,
to experience life as God intended?

Do you? Do we?

🕊

Thoughts:

Setting aside the teachings or structure
of organized religion,
how do you truly feel and believe,

Who is God?

What is God?

Where is God?

🌷

Thoughts:

Who am I
in the eyes of myself?

In the eyes of others?

In the eyes of God?

🌱

Thoughts:

What will God do now?

What will love do now?

What will you do now?

❦

Thoughts:

It's Never Too Late

To read a book to a child
To smile at a lost friend
To forgive
To care about everyone
To hold someone's hand
To pray
To try again
To befriend an enemy
To have fun
To learn something new
To hug someone special
To say, I love you.

I love you.

There Is So Much

There is so much to witness beyond
The language, the gender,
The age, the experiences,
The color of skin, the social status.

There is so much to comprehend beyond
The level of education, the neighborhood,
The religious affiliation, the birth place of life,
The sexual preference, the political stances.

There is so much to embrace beyond
Someone's present journey
To the depth of each soul
And the love given by God
To all - to everything.

There is so much to appreciate beyond
That which defines our uniqueness,
Our equality, our love, our Oneness,
In life, in creation, in eternity.

Will Always Be

Empty in the togetherness of lost time
Is the wonder of the inward choices,
To be as one is born
Or to live as one is taught.

With all the beauty of our gifts
Is the reflection of the fear.
Are we truly part of the sacred truth,
Or will we be vanished beyond
The possibility of a chosen few?

I must tell you for I am sure,
God is not that way.
With the thought of eternity
Was the promise of life's first day
And all of God's creation
Will always be.

Let Me Be

Let me be the will of God,
Let me be.
Let me be the voice of reason,
Let me be.
Let me be the heart of passion,
Let me be.
Let me be the path to peace,
Let me be.
Let me be the song of sincerity,
Let me be.
Let me be the reflection of choice,
Let me be.
Let me be the silent soul,
Let me be.
Let me be the creator of love,
Let me be.
Let me be me.

www.ingramcontent.com/pod-product-compliance
Lightning Source LLC
Chambersburg PA
CBHW031151090426
42738CB00008B/1289